# GETTING STARTED WITH CHICKS

First and foremost buy quality chicks directly from the hatchery or feed store.
We've raised heavy breeds, sometimes called 'dual purpose chickens':
Orpington, Barred Rock, Rhode Island Red, and Wyandotte. They produce
plenty of eggs for a home flock. These breeds, raised for meat production,
don't grow at a rate that makes them profitable. The feed conversion of grain
consumption to meat production doesn't make them an economical choice.
However, for beautiful, healthy, brown egg layers they're perfect. Sex Link
chicks grow into prolific egg layers. They are a lighter breed than the dual
purpose, but you're guaranteed to get hens, not roosters. Hatcheries have an
85% success rate in correctly identifying pullet chicks (female) from cockerel
chicks (male). Sex Link females hatch a different color than the male chicks
of the same breed, making them easily identified.

Before your chicks arrive, have your brooder area ready. For the brooder area, choose a draft free place. A garage, shed, barn, or basement will work. Set up a circular configuration for the chicks to prevent them from crowding into a corner and smothering. If you are brooding fifty chicks or less, a child's swimming pool works well. The sides are high enough that, for the first week or so, while the chicks are the most fragile, they're protected from drafts, overcrowding, or escaping. When chicks are two weeks old, remove the pool.

Now the chicks will have the larger brooder area. It needs to be draft free, hold a consistent temperature, and protect them from predators. Clean, dry bedding should cover the floor. Pine shavings work well; make sure you don't use sawdust which is very fine -- chicks will eat it. Spread pine shavings, at least 2 inches deep, throughout the area. Place heat lamps, hung from lightweight chain, so that a thermometer placed near the floor reads 95 degrees for the first week. Always have more than one lamp; if one goes out, your chicks still have a heat source. Use lower wattage output heat bulbs to prevent fire. Never have the lamp too close to bedding and NEVER use straw for new chicks or when using heat lamps. Each week, raise the lamp so that the temperature near the brooder floor lowers by five degrees. After a few weeks (five or six, depending on the temperature outside the brooder), remove the heat source. The chicks will be hardened off by this time.

During the first week, check the temperature regularly and adjust the lamps if necessary. Regulating the temperature after the first week is easy; the chicks' behavior will tell you if they're comfortable. When the chicks are huddled under the lamp, the brooder is too cold. The chicks should be scattered throughout the brooder and active. If all the chicks are making a ring on the outside of the lamp's circle, the lamp is too low and needs to be raised.

Space water and feed so that all chicks have access without crowding. Have more than one waterer and feeder. Place them away from the heat source (plastic will melt) and the water will be to warm. Quart jar style waterers work well, are easy to clean, are not too deep, and won't tip over easily. There are a variety of feeders designed especially for raising chicks. Hanging feeders should hang low enough for all the chicks to reach. If you have one use caution: chicks can get underneath and suffocate when surrounded by other chicks.

Keep the feed trays and water clean. Always give chicks tepid water, never cold water. When you first introduce your chicks to the brooder dip their beaks in water to teach them to drink. You can add electrolytes or vitamin supplements, specifically made for poultry, to their drinking water, but it isn't necessary. There's one ingredient that's very important for the chick's health: raw, apple cider vinegar (un-filtered, non-pasteurized like Bragg's brand). Adding one tablespoon per gallon of water prevents manure compaction and pasting of the chicks vent.

After five days, but NOT before, a couple drops of cod liver oil added to their drinking water, prevents leg problems. Don't over supplement with cod liver oil -- only a couple of drops give all the added vitamin D3 needed. Even better than cod liver oil... sunshine. Get the birds outside when they're feathered out and as soon as the weather permits.

NEVER let your chicks run out of water. Chickens consume twice the amount of water as food. Always keep the bedding dry. Remove wet bedding under or around water stations and replace it with dry bedding.

# SUITABLE HOUSING

The design of the coop determines the environmental conditions that will protect the birds. Ideal conditions inside the coop are important. If the poultry house is damp, drafty, cool, or poorly lighted, disease and poor health result. The following are essential for a healthy environment:

1. Dryness

2. Plenty of sunlight (artificial lighting is fine for a few weeks, but sunlight is important)

3. Ventilation without drafts

4. Plenty of floor space

5. Protection from excessive cold/heat

6. Rat and vermin proof construction

A healthy environment is one of the greatest factors in successfully raising chickens. It is the healthy, contented, well fed, singing hen that lays well. A good start insures success from the beginning.

For the small, backyard flocks, a coop built inside a garage or shed is a great alternative to a free-standing building, but remember, hens need outdoor access, too.

# Brooder Choices:

## The Swimming Pool Brooder

A brooder is an area set aside for newly hatched chicks. It must keep them warm, dry, draft free, and safe from predators. There are several styles of brooder.

A brooder made by using a child sized swimming pool works great for starting chicks. The round configuration keeps them from crowding into corners and suffocating. Here's how to set up a swimming pool brooder:

- cover bottom of pool with 2" of pine shavings
- Use 2 heat lamps (always have more than one source of heat in case one lamp burns out)
- Hang the lamps so the temperature at the floor is 95 degrees

- Set up water (never place it under the heat lamp)

- Set up feeder ((never place it under the heat lamp)

- NEVER use straw with a heat lamp -- there's a huge fire issue. Straw is not for chicks (it can cause leg issues)

- Check the temperature daily; 95 degrees the first week, cut 5 degrees each week afterwards

## BLACK TUB BROODER

An alternative to the child's swimming pool is to use a recycled protein tub or muck bucket. With a few simple changes the chicks have a warm area that allows them the freedom to enter and exit as they please. Keep the water and food outside the black tub. The tubs will keep the chicks warm. About twelve chicks will be comfortable inside a black tub. When the chicks feather out, or the outside temperature is warm enough, remove the tubs. Low wattage heat lamps, hung from a light weight chain, will replace the black tubs and lights.

These brooders are economical and easy to make using recycled protein tubs, from cattle supplements, or muck buckets (or any large, round, tub-style container will work). The sides of the tub should be sturdy, thick plastic.

When making a brooder always cut more than one hole in the side of the tub. Multiple holes give chicks easy entry and exit into the brooder. If just one hole is used, the chicks might pile up, blocking other chicks from entering or exiting. This could cause suffocation. Also, with only one entrance, too much heat could build up. With inadequate ventilation, both humidity and/or ammonia build-up causes health problems.

Pine shavings will cover the floor of the chicken area, and the black tubs will sit on top of the shavings. If the floor under the shavings is concrete, use 3 inches of shavings to cover the concrete floor. Think about it this way: with a heat source above them and a cold floor below them, the chicks' feet will radiate the cold up through their body. They will have difficulty maintaining their body temperature.

Here are the steps for making a black tub brooder:

***The black tub will be turned upside down, inside of the chicken pen. See pictures***

- Measure a lamp reflector
- Using a saw, cut a large hole in the bottom of the tub (the size of the lamp reflector).
- Cut 3 or 4 holes, close to the top, in the side of the tub 4" diameter.
- Use an incandescent bulb, NEVER use a heat lamp in this style brooder.
- Incandescent bulbs give off heat; use a 100 watt bulb the first week
- Place the tub style brooder inside the coop with water and food closely located outside the tub

Depending on the weather/temperature outside the brooder  lower the wattage of the lamp each week. For example: After a week or two switch from a 100 watt lamp to a 75 watt lamp. Use this lamp for a week or two. Lower the wattage until you can eliminate the heat source entirely once the birds are feathered out.

DO NOT use LED bulbs - they don't give off heat.

**Remember this rule of thumb:**

95 degrees for the first week, lower the temperature by 5 degrees each week until chicks are feathered out and the outside temperature is comfortable.

**Watering chicks**

- Use tepid water, never cold
- Introduce chicks to water before feed
- Never run out of water
- Keep bedding dry under water fountains

- Clean water daily
- Don't place water under heat source
- Use water fountains that won't tip over and are NOT more than 1" deep
- One gallon for every 12-15 hens daily
- Add a few drops of cod liver oil to increase vitamin D (after 5 days, NEVER before)
- Apple cider vinegar (raw, organic) prevents chicks from having pasting of the vent and manure build up causing impaction.

**Feeding Chicks**

- Use commercial starter feed for at least the first three days.
- Keep feed dry.
- Never use moldy feed.

• Starting on day four introduce chicks to green feeds (in addition to regular rations).

• Keep feeders off the ground at a height that prevents litter from getting into the feed.

• Remove un-eaten food from feeder daily. Feed only what they'll eat in a day.

• Never pour fresh feed into feeder with uneaten feed.

• Chicks need high protein  (21%); as they mature into laying hens, they need 16% protein

• Provide grit (appropriately sized), free choice

• Oyster shell, offered free choice - not mixed into the feed. Commercial layer rations have calcium carbonate mixed in for shell quality.

• Diatomaceous earth, kelp, and raw apple cider vinegar; all add to chick and hen's health

For the first few days use a complete commercial chick starter. After the first few days some families make their own feed using mixed grains. Remember chicks need small particle sized feed and a complete ration for ideal growth. I would suggest feeding a commercial ration. Look for organic, non- GMO, or at least non-medicated feed. If you decide to make your own laying hen feed remember that corn isn't the best feed choice, it's low in protein and high in fat; also, it's not easy finding non-GMO or organic corn. Wheat is a great alternative. Grains should be ground or milled. Whole grains will fill the croup, causing the birds to eat less, whole grain might cause impaction. Whole grains are fine as scratch grains for mature hens, not chicks, but they should not be the total diet of the chicken. Have grit available, free choice, not mixed in with feed rations.

Proteins, greens, and kitchen scraps (including meat scraps if insects aren't available) offer a balanced diet. If you have a source for raw milk, feed it to the chicks separately from dry feed and water. Don't feed more milk than the birds can finish within fifteen minutes. The lactic acid present in raw milk acts as an internal disinfectant. It's also a natural parasitic.

Chickens should have access to range outdoors and consume a variety of meat type proteins from insects. During the winter months, occasionally feeding laying hens meat scraps of raw, organic liver is a great supplement to their diet. Chickens are not vegetarians; they need meat protein to thrive. Organic liver is full of vitamins, minerals, enzymes and powerful nutrients without having filtered toxic substances from the host animal's diet.

Introduce fresh greens to the chicks after a few days in the brooder. The greens should be chopped fine or rough cut in a food processor. Feed them separately from the dry feed. Sit back and enjoy the show; when you first introduce greens one brave chick will be the first to try them. She'll loudly announce how delicious they are. The other chicks will decide they want what she has, only they won't go for the chopped greens in the feeder, they'll go for what she's carrying in her beak. They'll chase her around the brooder trying to steal her prize. Eventually they'll all settle down and start scratching through the greens themselves. It's very entertaining, and cheep fun, sorry for the pun!

Chicks mature rapidly. Within days of hatching, they'll begin growing pin feathers. If you are using a child's swimming pool, or a circular barrier inside the brooder, it can be removed when all the chicks have pin feathers. Remove the black tub style brooder a week or so later. The chicks will have the full range of the brooder area now, but they still need a heat source. In four weeks the chicks no longer need daytime heat, but on cold nights keep the heat lamps on. Use your best judgment when considering outdoor temperature.

# Germinated Oats or Seed

In the winter months feeding germinated oats provides enzymes for the hens. Germinated seed does not substitute for the loss of fresh greens, but the digestive enzymes in the germinated seed will help the hens derive more nutrients from their other feed sources.

When oats are soaked in water for about four days, a white tap root will sprout. The tap-root is the first kind of life that emerges from the seed. The young root and young germ -- as long as the germ remains white, and only half an inch long -- contains enzymes. The enzymes have digestion qualities that make vitamins and minerals in the feed more available.

When oats sprout into green shoots they're sprouted, offering different qualities than germinated seed. There's a distinct difference between feeding germinated and sprouted oats. Sprouted oats grow past the root and germ stage. During the sprouting process the valuable enzymes are used up by the sprouts; so they're lost to the poultry.

**Fodder**

Growing fodder is easy, fast and a great source of high protein feed. One pound of seed grows into 6 pounds of fresh green feed. Thirty-percent of a chicken's diet should be fresh greens. Greens reduce feed costs, and boosts vitamin D, Omega 3, CLA, Carotinoids, and other important vitamins. Deep rooted plants; like alfalfa, comfrey, and clover provide minerals and rich nutrients into the poultry's diet. Leafy greens improve the quality of hen health and eggs.

Typically, fodder is sprouted barley seed. It's grown for between seven and ten days. Other grains can be sprouted, but the protein level will be different. NEVER sprout tomato, eggplant or any nightshade seeds.

Here are the steps to follow:

- Soak seed for 12 hours in a mild bleach solution, 1 part bleach to 10 parts water.
- After soaking drain for 12 hours. Spread seed out on a flat bottomed plastic tray.

- The tray needs drainage holes at one end or use a tray that is open ended.

- Angle the tray so it slopes 1" for every 4 feet of length. Be sure to have a bucket to collect run-off.

- Water the seed 4 times per day or set up a misting system.

- Use a fan to circulate the air around the trays to inhibit mold growth.

- Baking Powder (potassium bicarbonate), one TBS/gallon of water inhibits mold growth or a mild solution of hydrogen peroxide can be used.

- Sprouted barley is 26% protein.

## Other Green Feed

Green feed can come from crops of clover, alfalfa, oats, grasses, or other greens -- leafy, succulent crops which can be easily grown. It's best to let chickens forage these themselves, but they can easily be cut and fed fresh during warm weather or dried for winter feeding.

## Plants for Chicken's Health

The plants that make up your lawn are great for grazing chickens, provided there aren't pesticides and herbicides being applied. Plant diversity will give greater health benefits. What might be viewed as weeds are actually beneficial to the health of your poultry. Plants with the deepest roots are generally higher in mineral content than shallow rooted varieties. Clover and alfalfa are high in calcium, phosphorus, vitamins A and D.

**<u>Spring Green Mix</u>**: This is the perfect mix for frost seeding; Mammoth Red Clover, Essex Dwarf Rape, and oats. In late February or early March scatter the seed over the ground. Snow covering the ground? No problem, these seeds work into the ground as it thaws. If you'd prefer to wait until warmer weather that is fine, too. Just rake or till a small plot, broadcast the seed, lightly rake to cover, and water. This is a highly nutritious mix to boost the protein content of green feed in your chicken yard. The oats will not go to seed head if they're grazed by the birds before maturity. These annuals will germinate quickly and be ready to graze in 4-6 weeks. For fall forage, use the following mix.

**<u>Fall Green Mix</u>**: This is a perfect blend of green feed for transitioning into the cool season of fall. Cereal Rye, Essex Dwarf Rape, and Buckwheat. Over seed with the mix in mid-July for early September foraging. Rake or till a small plot, broadcast the seed, lightly rake to cover, and water. Because you're seeding at the driest time of year scattering a light covering of straw over the freshly seeded area helps retain moisture. Water the straw regularly. When the seed germinates the straw breaks down into mulch adding organic matter to the soil.

# GARDENS FOR HEN HEALTH

The same plants grown in your family garden are ideal for feeding to your hens. Excess greens, squash, and tomatoes all benefit your hens. In the fall let your hens scratch through the fallen produce in your garden. They'll eat the seed, fruit, and insects. In the spring they'll scratch up the topsoil, fertilize, and eat early germinating weeds.

**Diatomaceous Earth (DE)**: Diatomaceous Earth is a natural pest control and parasitic. It cleanses internally and keeps your chickens free of external parasites. Use food grade DE. Added to your chickens feed it prevents caking and controls internal parasites. Used as a dust bath your hens will be happy and pest free. DE also controls algae in waterers. Add about one tablespoon per gallon of water to control algae growth.

**Raw Apple Cider Vinegar:** This is one of the most beneficial additives for chickens or any livestock for that matter. Added to drinking water it keeps your hens stress free, improves feed digestion, repels flies, lowers gut PH, and kills harmful bacteria. It also prevents manure build-up in the vents of chicks. Use 1 TBS per gallon of water.

**Cod Liver Oil:** Cod liver oil provides vitamin D, which prevents leg problems. A few drops added to drinking water will increase leg strength. The best source of vitamin D is sunshine, but young chicks need it before they're old enough to get outdoors. **Do Not** add cod liver oil until the chicks are at least five days old. Add it to one water fountain only. When the chickens have emptied it, clean it thoroughly.

**Kelp:** Kelp contains more than 53 trace minerals, amino acids, and vitamins. Buy naturally dried, OMRI approved kelp. It increases yolk quality. It's an important additive for hens health.

**Comfrey:** Both the leaves and root of comfrey can be used. The leaves should be harvested before the plant blossoms. Nutritional and medicinal values decline after blooming. Comfrey leaves are used in healing broken bones, cuts, burns and swellings. Comfrey is the only known land plant that contains vitamin B-12. It's also a good source of lysine, calcium, potassium, phosphorus, trace minerals, and amino acids. The leaves are rich in Vitamins A and C. Fresh leaves can be fed free choice to chickens. This is a deep rooted perennial that will spread, plant in an area where you can control its growth.

**Grit:** Grit is essential for digestion, it grinds feed in the chicken's crop, preventing impaction. Grit should be the appropriate size for your hens; larger grit for larger birds, starter grit for young chicks. Offered 'free choice' hens will get just what they need. Offer it separately, not mixed with feed.

**<u>B Vitamins</u>**: Every now and again we have a chick or a full grown hen whose neck and head are crooked. This particular chick was in the brooder when I noticed that she wasn't moving to the feeder with the rest of the flock. Usually, as soon as the feeders are re-filled, the chicks crowd around them. I noticed her head was tilted at a sharp angle - almost upside down. I gave her a quick exam; she hadn't been smothered, crushed, or stepped on. I placed her in a small bucket with shavings to cushion her and got out the bottle of B-12 vitamins.

If you ever find one of your poultry with this condition here are the steps to follow:

- Use B-12, Sub-lingual drops.

- Use a separate eye dropper to administer B-12 (you don't want to contaminate the bottle with bacteria)

- Pour some of the B-12 into a dish, using an eye dropper or syringe (without the needle) to draw up the vitamins. A couple of drops are more than enough for a chick.

- Tilt back the chicks head, open up the beak and squeeze in the drops. Make sure the chick swallows them.

- Don't use more than 2 drops; we're trying to heal, not drown, the chick.

- Keep her in a small box or container that's open on top and place it in a safe area where dogs, cats, or other chickens can't bother her.

- Repeat the drops three times a day for a couple days.

Every few hours you should see improvement. After one dose her head and neck should start to return to normal. Give the chick water in the same method as the B-12 a couple times a day and offer a small amount of feed free choice.

If you don't have B-12 raw, organic liver works, too. It's not as easy to use as the B-12 drops. Only feed organic liver or grass-fed liver. Otherwise you're feeding heavily toxic meat, the liver is a filter for toxins. Conventionally raised beef is full of additives that compromise the liver. Organic liver is full of vitamins and minerals. Organic livestock don't have toxins to contaminate their organ meat. Chop the liver very fine or use a food processor to make a paste. Open the chick's beak and feed a small amount of liver. Massage the chick's throat to make sure she doesn't choke. Follow this with a couple drops of water. It will take longer for the liver feeding to correct the crooked neck than the B-12 drops. You should see improvement within a couple of days.

## Chick Behavior

The best way to tell if your chicks are thriving is through observation. Chicks are fascinating to watch. You'll start to see 'the pecking order' in no time. You'll also learn early on to identify their sounds. Loud chirping is an alarm cry, usually to attract the mother hen (which in this case is you). Content, quiet chirping is conversational chatting among the flock. Loud chirps can indicate that the chicks are cold or that one has gotten outside the brooder.

Chicks mature rapidly. Within days of hatching they'll begin getting pin feathers. The circular barrier configuration in the brooder can be removed after ten days when all the chicks have pin feathers. The chicks will have the full range of the brooder area now. In four weeks the chicks no longer need daytime heat but on cold nights you may want to keep the heat lamps on, depending on the outdoor temperature.

## Chickens Come Home to Roost

By four weeks the chicks begin to roost. Set up a roost using wooden rod 2-3 inches in diameter. An old wooden ladder, with round rungs, hung from chains, works well. Use bracing to prevent it from swinging. As the chickens grow raise it to the proper height. Full grown, heavy breed chickens roost from 2 – 4 feet off the floor. Bantams will roost in rafters if they don't have a roost in the coop. The lighter breeds are able to roost higher up, a four foot high roost works well and will prevent them from roosting higher.

# Hardening Off Process

Getting the chicks in condition for the range starts the second week in the brooder. To harden-off gradually lower the temperature, with the idea of doing away with artificial heat entirely, after about six weeks for laying hens. This process depends on weather conditions, if you're raising spring chicks the best practice is to cut the artificial heat until it can be given up. Gradually allow more natural fresh air to enter the area until it can be entirely opened. It's impractical to take chickens from a warm, heated brooder house, and put them directly into outdoor pens. They need to be gradually acclimated to the change.

This hardening-off process is especially important because close feathering makes hens susceptible to cold weather. When not properly weaned of heat the hens pile on top of one another for warmth. When the hens are hardened off they can go out and range. The goal is for continuous growth throughout the summer. There are two factors, besides their inherited characteristics, which affect proper maturity. They are; environmental conditions and food supply.

Environment plays an important part in growing healthy chickens. The best bred hens, if not given ideal conditions, will not grow or develop to the fullest extent. The following are essential:

1. Allow the hens ample area to range. Never keep hens in confinement.

2. Sunshine with access to shade should be provided.

3. An abundance of green succulent food is necessary.

4. Fresh air, without drafts, and clean, dry bedding are necessary.

Feeding isn't complicated, complete feed should be used. Offering a variety of foods to the hens helps them balance their own diet.

During the summer months, when the birds are outdoors and able to range, their feed ration can be cut back as long as there are plenty of legumes and insects for supplementation.

**Nesting Boxes**

Nesting boxes should be in place by the time the hens are three months old. The hens will begin laying when they're between 5 and 7 months old. Before the onset of laying, the hens will practice nesting. Straw or soft wood shavings should line the nesting boxes. Clean nesting boxes mean clean eggs; Keep the hens out of the boxes at night.

Nesting boxes should have a top that slopes to prevent the hens from roosting on top of them. They're easy to build, if you're handy with tools, anyway. Otherwise search farm sales for nesting boxes. Milk crates work. Attach them to the wall and make a top board to keep the chickens from roosting on them at night.

Nesting boxes should be 12 - 18 inches above the floor. Some hens like to lay their eggs under the nesting box instead of inside. As long as the bedding is clean under the boxes the eggs will be fine. Hens don't like having their eggs taken, they'll hide them. You can trick them by using wooden or ceramic eggs, placed in the nesting boxes, to encourage the hens to lay there. When there's an egg inside the box the hen will decide it's a safe place to lay. They'll lay their eggs next to the fake egg, keeping you from having to search for hidden nests.

# Buying Juvenile Hens

An alternative to raising chicks is to buy juvenile hens, ready to lay. Find a reliable farm that raises free range chickens, fed a healthy diet of non-GMO or organic grains and greens and absolutely no antibiotics. If chickens are properly raised there's no need for antibiotics in their feed or water. If you are buying hens be sure they have been given access to outdoor areas and haven't been raised in cages. Caged chickens will have underdeveloped legs, and a diminished capacity to forage. Also, they may have been de-beaked, which means their top beak is cut back by nearly half its length, the lower beak is also trimmed short. De-beaking is done in confinement facilities to discourage hens from pecking each other and to prevent feed waste. If chickens are raised properly there's no need to mutilate them. De-beaking is a mutilation performed because the living conditions are stressful and overcrowded. Confinement housing, without outdoor access, is an unnatural environment.

Pullets mature into laying hens at between 5-7 months. If you buy chicks in the spring you'll be waiting months for eggs. In the fall, when they finally start laying, the decreasing daylight hours will trigger the hens to start going into a dormant cycle. Unless artificial lighting is provided they may not start laying until the following spring. Also, by starting with young hens you won't be surprised when one of your pullets turns out to be a rooster, this is fairly common when buying chicks. The hatcheries have an 85% accuracy rate with identifying the sex of chicks. Unless you are buying a 'sex link' breed there's no guarantee the chick is a hen instead of a rooster.

# Outdoor Pens And Yards

Weather permitting, the birds can be moved to their outdoor coop or given access to an outdoor range, if that's the plan for your flock. Outdoor access is essential to the health of the hen. The quality of her eggs improve and the benefits to both yard and garden are clear by thriving, pest free, plants. If you are using a mobile coop move it every day to prevent manure build up. If the hens have a range area, accessed by a door from inside the coop, divide the range into at least four separate sections. The hens rotate through each section, allowing re-growth before the hens graze it again. The coop should have access doors opening into each different area of their range. When one plot is not being used keep that access door closed. Plant each area with a variety of vegetation. The consumption of commercial feed becomes less once the hens forage outdoors. Supplementing their diet with kitchen scraps, bread and vegetable waste adds feed value.

Chickens need protection from predators whether they are in the coop, yard, or free ranging. Rats and mice are attracted to chicken feed. Store it in metal garbage cans with the lids tightly secured. Rats kill young chicks. They can wipe out your flock in one night. A rat can fit through very small openings, the size of a quarter, and climb through narrow gaps.

Other predators include weasel, owls, hawks, raccoons, foxes, dogs, and cats. A weasel will suck the blood out of a chick or full-grown hen. Both weasel and owl take the entire head and leave the carcass behind. Owls are stealth, they hunt at night when your chickens are paralyzed by night blindness. Secure the hens at night, closing the coop doors and windows.

Don't overlook your pet dog as a possible predator. Some dogs kill chickens for sport.

Our dogs are raised with poultry. They're taught to respect all of the livestock. Occasionally visitors to the farm will bring their dog along for the ride. They always assure us that their dog would never bother the chickens or other farm animals. Nine times out of ten, they're wrong.

We keep a few geese at the farm for protection. Geese are curious and territorial. One hen's alarm cry sends all the chickens running for safety. The geese, attracted by the cries, come to investigate.

When the offending dog spots a few fat geese moving slowly through the barnyard it decides the geese are easier to catch than the chicken. Going after a goose is a big mistake. Geese are great at teaching farm etiquette to ill-behaved dogs. The geese will give the dog a warning hiss, then, with their necks outstretched, the geese charge forward to surround the dog. If he's persistent, or doesn't recognize the threat, he'll continue going after the geese. When they've had enough the geese will grab the dog by the scruff of the neck and beat it with their wings.

The dog, trying to escape, will pull back. The geese will move forward in unison, not letting go until the dog is on the ground. They'll continue circling the dog, beating, hissing, and grabbing even more flesh. When they believe the dog has learned its lesson they'll release it.

We've never had a dog go after the geese -- or hens for that matter -- a second time. Usually the dog ends up cowering at its master's feet or hiding under their car.

# FORCED MOLT

*"If birds of a feather flock together what do naked birds do?"*

The hen molts when she quits laying and she quits laying when she runs out of the necessary elements to make an egg. That is why some hens molt early - - poor nutrition.

The longer daylight hours, flush of warm weather, and fresh greens stimulate the hen to lay heavily in the spring. As summer progresses towards fall the vital nutrients in her diet diminish. The shorter daylight hours combined with her depleted diet leave the hen without the necessary elements to continue laying. Once she stops laying her body begins the molting process. Hens that molt early usually have poor nutrition.

Molting is a natural process, unless there are extenuating circumstances, allow hens to cycle through egg production naturally. Allowing hens to molt naturally is the best option. You're raising backyard birds - not high production, commercial flocks, which, by the way, cull hens after one year. There's no value in the commercial flock once they molt, so they're culled at one year. If you're concerned about natural molting during the coldest months of winter you might try forcing hens to molt earlier. This will give the hens time to grow new feathers before the dead of winter. In August or September you can force molt. Diminishing daylight hours and cooler temperatures, along with dietary changes will trigger the pituitary gland to slow hormone production.

These are the steps to follow:

- Close your hens in an indoor coop.
- Turn the lights off for three days (a night light is fine but nothing brighter than 25 watts)
- Provide clean water but no food ( for three days).

- After three days feed a reduced ration that's lower in protein.
- Keep the lights dim
- This stress will induce molting.
- Hens will begin loosing feathers.
- Use a red light bulb, not a heat lamp, to prevent cannibalism.
- The molting process will take twenty-one days.

Following the twenty-one days of low lighting, reduced feed, and feather loss, increase light (both wattage and by extending lighting hours). Lights should be kept on for twelve to fourteen hours per day. Increase the protein content of the feed and begin feeding greens. The greens can be fodder or fresh greens from gardens, yards, or lawn clippings (if chemical free). The combination of light and protein will stimulate hormone production. Egg laying will start again soon. The eggs will be fewer but larger during the hens second laying season. Be sure to offer grit, oyster shell, and diatomaceous earth.

**When molt occurs, either naturally or induced, a red light should be used to prevent cannibalism.**

**Molting hens will get pecked at by other curious hens. Feather loss exposes flesh that looks "pocked." The pocked skin resembles insects on the flesh which causes greater pecking behavior. If the pecking is severe, blood is drawn, triggering even more pecking. A red lamp (bulb), NOT a heat lamp, will alter the hen's vision enough to end this behavior.**

# WHAT TO DO WITH ALL THE EGGS

Start collecting egg recipes! Hens lay five - seven eggs per week, depending on the breed you're raising. Selling eggs is a great business for kids. Raising laying hens teaches children responsibility, economics, and good business practices. When our sons were young they were responsible for feeding and watering the chickens. They collected and washed the eggs. When they were a little older, they sold eggs and donated a third of their eggs to the local food pantry. The cartons included a chicken joke or fun fact about chickens. Twice a year a newsletter, placed in the carton, shared information about their chickens. Their marketing worked -- they had a waiting list for eggs, learned to give, and increased the flock to keep up with demand.

## More Benefits of Raising Hens

If you're a gardener chicken composted manure is a great source of nitrogen. The key is to compost it for at least one year before adding it to the garden. The ammonia in fresh chicken manure can burn plants.

Enjoy having chickens in your yard working for you. They'll keep the garden clean and pest free. Hens work for food; they eat kitchen scraps, extra veggies from the garden and pests. Even better, you'll have fresh eggs daily! Hens are economical and great recyclers. They'll turn vegetable waste into eggs and fertilizer.

# A Word of Caution before Raising Chickens:

## Chickens - The Marijuana Of Livestock

If marijuana is a gateway drug, then chickens are the marijuana of livestock. The natural progression of small acreage farming goes something like this...

You dig up an area in your yard to start a garden. After the first season some laying hens are brought in to clean and fertilize it. They'll do a great job keeping weeds and insects under control.

In return, they'll give you a fresh egg every day. With an abundance of fresh veggies and eggs you'll feel peace and happiness that you've never known before.

When another season has passed you'll start searching for more areas to enlarge your garden space. The bigger garden will get you thinking more about soil health and composting.

You'll read an old garden book from the golden age of farming. It will praise pigs as a great tilling and fertilizing tool. Farmers of old turned a few feeder pigs into the garden to clean it up.

Before long you'll be looking for a place to raise a pig. If you're lucky you'll find a little piece of land in the country where you can have a couple of pigs.

The pigs will eat your garden waste, till the land in the fall, and feed your family the best meat you've ever tasted. Before long you'll start dreaming of adding a dairy goat or house cow. The fresh milk will feed your family, the excess milk will feed the chickens and pigs. The eggs will get even better and the pork will be outstanding.

Just think, it all started with a chicken, which, by the way, is why I call them the marijuana of livestock!

9 798452 932642